THE LIE
WITHIN THE
LIGHT

Tom,

Your questions challenged me to search deeper and think harder. Your questions not only provided the insight that led to this book, but I answer one specifically in the last chapter.

Thank you for asking, not dictating.

Author's Note:

This book is not meant as a showcase of my writing ability. My goal has never been to elevate myself as a writer, but to lift up the Word of God.

While I guided, directed, and reviewed every word to ensure it aligns with Scripture, I also used modern tools, including AI, to help shape and refine the text. The heart, message, and testimony are mine; the tools simply helped me communicate them more clearly and efficiently.

I am not a professional writer by trade. I am an IT manager, a husband, and a father of three. Most of my days begin at 5 a.m. and end late. After work, I have enough time for family, dinner, and the Word right before bed. The only reason this book was completed is because of a brief paternity leave that gave me the space to pour into it. Now that I am back in the daily grind, my writing will naturally slow.

If the thought that not every sentence was typed by my own hand troubles you, then perhaps this book is not for you. But if you can receive it for what it truly is, my testimony, my direction, and my heart to point people to Christ, then this book is for you.

Table of Contents

Scripture quotations are taken primarily from the New International Version (NIV), which is in the public domain.

ISBN 979-8-9999932-2-9
Printed in the United States of America.

Introduction

This book isn't for the perfect. It's for the searching.

It's for those who have whispered prayers into the silence and wondered if anyone was listening.

For those wounded by religion, carrying scars from church pews instead of the world; for those who grew up with rules but never encountered love. For those who tried their best and still felt like it wasn't enough.

It's for the ones caught in deception and who don't yet know it. For those chasing light, only to find that not all light is good. Those who are spiritually curious, hungry, and unsure: for the ones who ache for truth but can't quite put words to the longing.

It's also for the Pharisee. The rule-follower. The one bound by religion, not relationship, who may know Scripture but has yet to meet the Savior behind the words.

It's for the ones who once believed but walked away… and for the ones who never believed but can't ignore the pull inside their chest.

If you've ever wondered if God still speaks, if He still sees, if He still saves, this book is for you.

You don't have to agree with everything in these pages. You don't have to come with clean hands or a polished faith. Just come with an open heart.

Because if you seek Him, not religion, not philosophy, not a feeling, but *Him*, you will find Him.

And when you do, everything changes.

Prologue: The Pattern That Fooled Me

I didn't write this book because I had all the answers. I wrote it because I had been fooled.

For years, I pursued truth with a sincere heart. I wanted to understand God and live a life filled with purpose and light. And what I found looked good. It sounded spiritual. It gave me a framework, a community, even a sense of mission. But over time, something didn't sit right. Not in a loud, dramatic way, but more like subtle, unsettling cracks beneath the surface.

I had unknowingly stepped into a belief system that claimed to be of God but redefined who Jesus is.

What started as confidence turned into confusion. I noticed a pattern, a familiar script seen in belief systems across cultures and generations. They often offer hidden knowledge, personal empowerment, or enlightenment. They might quote Scripture, invoke the name of Jesus, or speak of light and angels. But when examined closely, they share one fatal flaw:

They distort, diminish, or replace the true identity of Christ.

That's how deception works. It doesn't require you to reject God outright. It just needs you to believe in a version of Him that isn't true.

So, I stepped back quietly, gradually, from a belief system that once gave structure to my entire life. I'm not naming it here. That's not out of avoidance but out of love for those still within it. My aim isn't to provoke or divide. It's sharing what I see and inviting others to seek God with fresh eyes.

If you're reading this and sense something familiar in my story, lean in with prayer and discernment. The truth doesn't fear examination. Neither should we.

If you're in a system that adds to Christ, alters Him, or shifts the foundation away from the Word of God, this book is for you. I'm not asking you to follow me, just to examine what you believe.

Ask yourself:

Does my belief system exalt Christ as He is, or only as I've been told He is?

Does it align with the Word, or compete with it?

Here's the truth I had to face:

"In the beginning was the Word, and the Word was with God, and the Word was God."
— John 1:1

This Word isn't just divine. It is God.

Then we read:

"The Word became flesh and made his dwelling among us. We have seen his glory, the glory of the one and only Son, who came from the Father, full of grace and truth."

— John 1:14

Let that sink in. The Word, described in verse 1 as being God, became flesh in verse 14.

That's when it all came together: The Word, who is God, became flesh.

God became Jesus in the flesh.

And to remove all doubt, verse 17 names Him directly:

"For the law was given through Moses; grace and truth came through Jesus Christ."

— John 1:17

This isn't poetic symbolism. It's a clear, intentional progression.

Jesus is the Word. The Word is God. Jesus is God made flesh.

That truth shattered my illusions and rebuilt my foundation.

And when that truth moved from my head to my heart, when I truly met Him, everything changed.

He entered my spirit. My cup overflowed. I craved Him. I longed to know Him. My heart yearned to hear His voice and stay near His presence. Scripture stopped being an obligation. It became oxygen.

All I wanted was clear communication with the living God.

And then something happened, something I never could've made happen through effort or willpower alone.

There was a sin I had carried since high school. A stronghold. An addiction. A hidden weight I had begged God for years to remove. I fasted. Practices extensive self-discipline. And failed. But the day I met Him, it left. Instantly. Completely. Quietly.

Not because I tried harder, but because I finally came to the One who could carry it for me.

"Come to me, all you who are weary and burdened, and I will give you rest. Take my yoke upon you and learn from me, for I am gentle and humble in heart, and you will find rest for your souls. For my yoke is easy and my burden is light."
— Matthew 11:28–30

He wasn't offering rules. He was offering Himself.

Before this encounter, I thought going to church was the point. Follow the rules, check the boxes, be good enough, and hope it all works out. But once I met Him, I realized it was never about checking boxes.

It was about knowing Him. About knowing His Word.

Here's the "catch"

Once the Spirit is in your heart, you desire the house of worship. You crave it. Not because you're trying to earn anything, but because your soul has tasted the goodness of God, and you can't get enough. Though your cup is spilling over, you still thirst for more.

"As the deer pants for streams of water, so my soul pants for you, my God. My soul thirsts for God, for the living God."
— *Psalm 42:1–2*

Now, looking back, I see how deeply I once lived in bondage. I never felt like I could measure up. No matter how hard I tried, I always fell short. I carried shame, self-doubt, and a constant sense of unworthiness, the very strongholds Satan uses to keep people bound.

The truth is, I wasn't resting on the cross. I hadn't received what Jesus had already paid for.

When I finally surrendered, not to a system, but to a Savior, those chains broke.

And anything that contradicts this truth is, by definition, antithetical to God Himself. That realization changed everything.

So, before we dive in, I ask you to watch for the pattern. You'll see it show up again and again throughout this book. And more importantly, you may see it in places you never expected. If you do, don't run from it. Follow it. Expose it.

Once you see the lie for what it is, only then can you grasp the truth that sets us free.

"Then you will know the truth, and the truth will set you free."
— John 8:32

Let's begin.

Chapter 1: In the Beginning

Why This Chapter Comes First

There's a principle that says: before you can understand how or what, understand why. Without a clear sense of purpose, the rest is just noise.

This chapter isn't here to convince you of something. It's not a debate. It's the foundation. Because if we're going to talk about the lies hiding in the light, about the way truth can be twisted and deception can wear a holy mask, then we have to start by asking: What is actually true?

Without that foundation, the rest of this book won't mean much. Not because the content won't matter, but because you won't have the lens to see it clearly.

If the Prologue shared the heartbeat of why I wrote this book, then this chapter lays the bedrock.

So, before we expose what's false, let's look at what's real.

Where did it all begin?

"In the beginning, God created the heavens and the earth."
— *Genesis 1:1*

This is how the Bible begins, firm and unambiguous. A definitive claim of origin. Whether or not you believe it, the opening line of Genesis doesn't hesitate or hedge. It doesn't offer theories or speculation. It starts with certainty: there was a beginning, and God started it.

Now let's take a moment to talk about science.

People often misunderstand science as a source of truth, but by definition, science is not truth. Truth stands alone, unchanging, independent, and absolute. Truth is its own definition. Science is a process. It is a method of discovery, a systematic approach to understanding the natural world. It begins with a question or observation, proceeds through a hypothesis, and then enters the critical phase of experimentation. Through repeated testing and peer review, we gather evidence, not proof, but support for, or against a hypothesis. Theories may become widely accepted, but they are always subject to revision as new data emerges.

So, what happens when we apply this method to the biggest question of all: How did the universe begin? How did life come to be?

Astrophysicist Hugh Ross, who has spent decades studying the origin of the cosmos, points out that the Big Bang, while scientifically supported, still leaves us with a monumental question: What caused it? If time, space, matter, and energy all began at that singularity, then the cause must exist outside of time, space, matter, and energy. That's not just a theological assertion; it's a philosophical and scientific reality. Using the scientific method, we attempt to find natural explanations for natural phenomena. But when we apply that same lens to the origin of consciousness, the fine tuning of the universe, or the striking consistency in near death experience accounts across cultures, the evidence doesn't lead to a conclusion of no God, it reveals the outline of something, or Someone, beyond natural explanation.

In these spaces, where physics meets mystery, where brain scans meet soul questions, we encounter data that resists purely materialistic answers.

This chapter will walk through the evidence. Not dogma. Not blind faith. But reasoned arguments, rooted in logic, near-death accounts, and the ever-unfolding mystery of human experience.

Two modern investigators, Lee Strobel and John Burke, have approached these questions not as preachers or philosophers, but as skeptics willing to follow the evidence. Both came from a place of doubt. Both walked on the edge of disbelief. And both emerged deeply changed, not because of a spiritual encounter in a cave or a quiet epiphany in the woods, but because the data pointed somewhere they didn't expect.

Lee Strobel, a former atheist and investigative journalist for the Chicago Tribune, took on the question of miracles in his book The Case for Miracles. He approached it like a courtroom case: examine the witnesses, verify the documentation, and cross-examine the natural explanations.

One of the most striking cases he encountered was that of Barbara Cummiskey Snyder. Doctors had diagnosed Barbara with multiple sclerosis, so advanced that she was blind, dependent on a breathing tube, and expected to die at any moment. Medical records from the Mayo Clinic confirmed the diagnosis. But then, after a nationwide call for prayer, something happened that even her doctors couldn't explain. She felt a sudden rush of energy through her body, removed her breathing tube, stood up from her wheelchair, and could see again. Her muscles, long atrophied, regained strength immediately. And now, decades later, she's still fully healed. This wasn't an ambiguous "feeling better" story. The medical community documented and witnessed the lasting effects.

Cases like Barbara's challenge the boundaries of materialist explanations. Spontaneous recovery? Possibly. Misdiagnosis? Unlikely, given the clinical history. Coincidence? Maybe. But when something this precise, this medically improbable, and this directly tied to prayer occurs, many times over across various cultures, it begs the question: Are we seeing the fingerprints of something beyond?

If Strobel's investigation of miracles highlights the intervention of God in the physical, then John Burke's exploration of near-death experiences brings that same mystery into the spiritual. A former skeptic and engineer turned pastor, Burke compiled over a thousand NDEs from people of every background, atheists, Muslims, agnostics, and Christians, recording stories from around the globe. What struck him wasn't just the number of accounts, but their consistency.

Many of the people Burke interviewed described leaving their physical bodies and observing scenes around them with astonishing accuracy, sometimes recounting surgical procedures or family conversations they couldn't have witnessed. Others described encountering a radiant being of light, overwhelming in love and peace, whom many identified as Jesus, even when they came from non-Christian backgrounds.

One executive named "Randy," who had no interest in religion, clinically died and reported a vivid encounter with Christ. He came back changed. Not emotional. Not suggestible. But clear, direct, and altered. He knew things about the procedure and conversations that happened in the hospital room while he was dead, things he had no possible way of knowing.

These stories echo each other across geography, age, culture, and worldview. There are differences in symbolic language, but at the core, many describe the same experience: a deep sense of being known, a life review, and an encounter with a loving being who radiates light and truth. And it isn't always pleasant; some describe darkness, separation, even hellish realms that were only escaped through calling out to God.

Burke doesn't sensationalize these accounts. He investigates them, filters out weak or unverifiable claims, and compares them against Scripture. The result is a body of evidence that demands attention, not only because of the consistency, but because of the clarity it offers: death may not be the end. In fact, it may be a doorway.

Strobel and Burke do not present the testimonies here to force belief, but to reframe the question. If even one of them is true, then we're not just dealing with neurons and atoms. We're dealing with something personal. Something intentional. Something divine.

These miraculous and near-death accounts are not singular occurrences. They are part of a growing mosaic that suggests something deeper is going on behind the veil of our physical world. You don't have to be a theologian or a mystic to feel it, you just have to listen.

A woman on her deathbed sees her childhood friend waiting to greet her, someone no one knew had also just passed. A man blind from birth describes the layout of a hospital room after flatlining. A hardened skeptic experiences a sudden healing that even the attending physician calls "medically inexplicable." These stories don't demand belief. They invite curiosity. These stories awaken within us a feeling we often try to suppress for the sake of reason, that quiet, persistent sense of a greater purpose.

If you're looking for airtight formulas or a sterile chain of logic that leads you to God like a math problem, you won't find it here. The Spirit doesn't operate like data. We don't measure it, we are moved by it. It responds to beauty, to love, to truth that resonates too deep for words.

In this book, I'm not trying to win an argument. I'm offering a trail of clues. What you do with them is up to you.

The Prophetic Thread

But the trail doesn't end with miracles and near-death accounts. In fact, some of the most interesting evidence that God is not only real but intentional comes from history itself, through prophecy.

If we see God's fingerprints in moments of divine healing or glimpses beyond death, then prophecy is His handwriting, etched across time, through people, places, and promises fulfilled. Nowhere is this clearer than in the life of Jesus of Nazareth.

Even secular historians acknowledge Jesus was a real, historical figure. The question is not whether He existed, but who He was.

Prophets foretold His coming long before His arrival.

Centuries earlier, the prophet Isaiah described a coming servant who would suffer, be rejected, bear the sins of others, and yet somehow bring healing to the world. Isaiah 53 reads more like a biography of Christ than a vague poetic metaphor. It speaks of a man "pierced for our transgressions" and "crushed for our iniquities," whose punishment would bring us peace. The text was written roughly 700 years before Jesus' life.

Skeptics once claimed these were Christian insertions or later edits. But in 1947, people made an astonishing discovery: The Dead Sea Scrolls. Among them was a complete copy of the book of Isaiah, carbon-dated to more than a century before Jesus walked the earth. Word for word, it matches the text we have today. No edits. No revisions. The prophecy stood long before its fulfillment.

The statistical likelihood of a single man fulfilling at least eight significant Old Testament Messianic prophecies (many in Isaiah) has been computed by mathematician Peter Stoner. The probability? One in 10 to the 17th power. That's one in one hundred quadrillion. And Jesus fulfilled not just eight, but over three hundred.

The fingerprints become a signature.

And then there's the Shroud of Turin, perhaps the most mysterious relic in existence. Believed by many to be the burial cloth of Jesus, it bears the faint image of a crucified man. Not painted. Not stitched. Untouched by fire. The image behaves like a photographic negative, encoded with three-dimensional depth. High-resolution imaging and ultraviolet analysis allowed scientists to determine that only a burst of radiant energy could have formed the image. One study concluded that it would require a flash of light equivalent to several billion watts of ultraviolet radiation, something no technology on Earth can currently replicate.

And yet... there it is.

As if the resurrection left a calling card, not in myth, but in matter.

Some would say this is a coincidence.

But if it is, it's the most orchestrated coincidence the world has ever seen.

And if the story is true, if Jesus was more than a man, more than a prophet, more than a symbol, then maybe the most profound truth of all is this:

The Creator did not stay distant.

He stepped in.

Chapter Two: If I Were the Devil – Cultural & Religious Deception

"If I were the devil, I would whisper to you as I whispered to Eve: 'Do as you please.'"

— Paul Harvey, 1965

In that 1965 radio address, Paul Harvey imagined what Satan might do to corrupt a nation from within. He envisioned a slow, strategic unraveling, not by force, but by seduction. The devil wouldn't appear with horns and fire; instead, he'd slip through the cracks of culture, cloaked in convenience, pleasure, and false promises.

Targeting the youth, he'd distort the truth, teaching that the Bible is a myth and morality outdated. He'd lull the older generations into misplaced trust, redirecting prayers from heaven to the state. He'd hijack entertainment, education, and religion, polluting each pillar of society subtly, until no one noticed what was missing.

Harvey foresaw a future where churches prioritize popularity over holiness, classrooms cultivate intellect while neglecting the heart, and progress banishes God. The result? Families divided, truth redefined, and a generation so tranquilized by culture that it forgets its under attack.

In other words, if I were the devil, I'd just keep right on doing what he's doing.

This language, spoken roughly 60 years ago, makes a very important point: the devil does not approach people in an obviously evil manner; Scripture confirms this reality:

"And no wonder, for Satan himself masquerades as an angel of light."
— 2 Corinthians 11:14

"The great dragon was hurled down—that ancient serpent called the devil, or Satan, who leads the whole world astray."

— Revelation 12:9

He is the primary deceiver. The enemy's most successful schemes are not blatant; they are beautifully packaged lies, dressed in light, empathy, and half-truths.

Over time, I've come to recognize one of Satan's most effective tactics: he works with five truths and one lie. A single distortion slipped in among what feels familiar and trustworthy. But it's enough, a carefully placed fracture in the foundation that eventually brings the entire structure down. This is how he undermines not just individuals, but entire cultures, movements, and belief systems.

Throughout this book, we'll explore how Satan himself, just as Paul Harvey warned, manipulates churches, religions, and philosophies. These systems often share a common foundation: they acknowledge Jesus existed. But here's the catch: many subtly distort who He truly is.

That's the formula.

The pattern.

The lie within the light.

Where does that distortion lead?

We'll get there.

In the next chapter, I'll share how I fell into this distortion, and how it brought a peace that wasn't really peace at all.

Chapter Three: The Peace That Wasn't Peace – My Time in the New Age

After my brother passed away in 2023 at the young age of 29, I searched for answers with a desperation I'd never felt before. In my grief, I turned to near-death experiences (NDEs). What started as curiosity quickly became a spiritual pursuit. These stories led me to podcasts and voices in the spirituality community, people who spoke with a calm authority, blending science, metaphysics, and what sounded like biblical truth… but with a twist I'd never heard before. And it brought me peace.

For the first time in a long time, I felt relief. It was like someone had cracked open the sky and whispered, "You were right to hope for more."

I believed in heaven, prophecy, angels, and that Jesus was divine in some meaningful way, though not in the way I would come to understand later. My upbringing in a religious environment familiarized me with teachings suggesting more to reality than just the physical world, and it acknowledged miracles and God. That foundation gave me a framework that made what I encountered next feel familiar, even comforting.

Their conversation included God, energy, healing, and consciousness. They quoted Jesus. They referenced scripture lightly. But they added things. Things that weren't in the Bible but sounded good, even better. The message wasn't repent and believe; it was let go and grow. You don't need to worry about right or wrong; they said. You're just here to grow. Earth is a classroom. Everything is a lesson. In the end, we all return to the Light.

There was a softness to it all. No fear. No urgency. Just a gentle invitation to float downstream and trust the current.

There was no hell, they insisted. That was just religious trauma, an invention from Dante's Inferno or medieval control tactics. They rejected the idea of eternal judgment, calling it past fear-mongering. Now this… this was good news. My brother and I would both make it. There was no doubt, no judgment, just a universal consciousness awaiting us both.

And I believed it because I wanted to.

I wanted peace so badly, and this belief system gave it to me. It encouraged me to relax more, to not worry about anything. The more I listened, the more testimonies I heard. Some of these people took ayahuasca or DMT, having visions, speaking with "guides," getting answers to questions they'd carried for years. They claimed it wasn't just a hallucination, especially since some of them had used no psychedelics at all. These were real beings, giving real wisdom.

The way they described it — the colors, the warmth, the overwhelming sense of love — it made our physical world seem pale by comparison. Why would I question it when everything in me wanted it to be true?

I became interested in people like Joe Dispenza, who taught that through meditation and connecting with "universal energy," you could heal your body. Miracles were happening. Real ones. There were clinical studies. There was a documentary called Source that showed it happening. And I thought, this even touches the supernatural side of the God I believe in.

Soon, I was hearing testimonies of people with psychic abilities. They could see things about other people's lives. People practiced Reiki healing, channeling energy into others without touch. It seemed to work. They spoke of the law of attraction: that your thoughts and emotions emit vibrational frequencies that draw experiences back to you. Good energy brings excellent results. Manifestation is a spiritual principle. People even quoted scripture out of context to support it: "As a man thinketh, so is he."

It was as if something had thinned the veil between worlds, and I was finally entering a higher understanding. No more stale doctrine. No more shame. Just endless depth.

Everything I wanted in my old form of Christianity was here. It was mystical. Experiential. Inclusive. Powerful.

And it talked about Jesus… But not that Jesus.

This Jesus wasn't the Savior. He wasn't the Messiah, the Son of God. He was a teacher. A misunderstood guru. A messenger of unconditional love. That was the new gospel: love is god, not God is love.

And honestly? It felt amazing.

They were kind.

They were accepting.

They even performed miracles.

Surely, they were the ones who really understood Jesus… right?

Chapter Four: Cracks in the Light

In this spiritual circle, there were some who claimed to speak to angels. They called it "channeling." These were the same voices that loosely quoted Scripture, often out of context, but always in a tone that extended the kind of peace I was finding through the near-death experiences I'd been consuming.

I believed in a supernatural God. I believed in angels. That wasn't a stretch for me. My religious upbringing had already given me a framework where divine beings could interact with humanity. I was familiar with stories of people receiving visions, angelic visitations, or spiritual revelations. So, I wasn't alarmed when I heard New Age practitioners talk about receiving messages from angels or spirit guides during meditation.

I was familiar with adding to scripture. In my worldview ongoing revelation wasn't foreign; it was welcomed. So, when something was said through a "new lens" or "fresh download," I didn't question it. I accepted it as part of the spiritual evolution of truth. I thought: Maybe this is just another level of understanding.

But then, something subtle shifted.

As I consumed more and more of this content, I noticed contradictions. One person's "divine message" contradicted another's "truth." These contradictions weren't small; they were foundational. However, no one debated or reconciled them. People brushed aside those contradictions with the now-popular phrase: "Well, that's their truth."

The idea of "my truth" was everywhere. There was no absolute. No standard. Everything was fluid. One teacher believed reincarnation was real; another said it wasn't, but both were "right." After all, they said, we live in a multiverse, and there's growing evidence in quantum physics, specifically quantum entanglement, that all possibilities can coexist. This gave just enough of a scientific sheen to spiritual contradictions that it made it feel intelligent. Progressive. Enlightened. But deep down, something felt... off.

Outside of my spiritual journey, I would occasionally indulge in more grounded, worldly content, usually tied to my military background. One day, I tuned in to The Shawn Ryan Show, a podcast I respected for its raw honesty. The guest that day? Father Dan Reehil, a Catholic priest and exorcist. The podcast episode was called "Inside the Demonic World with an Exorcist" (SRS #141).

At first, I was just curious. It sounded entertaining. But what I heard shook me.

Father Reehil wasn't offering vague anecdotes. He was detailing real spiritual warfare, documented exorcisms. Accounts of people growling in voices not their own, speaking ancient languages they'd never studied, displaying inhuman strength, and revealing secrets about people in the room no one else could have known.

And then it hit me.

The way these demons manifested, speaking through the possessed, was disturbingly similar to what I had seen in the channeling community. There too, individuals would enter meditative states, sometimes aided by psychedelics, other times through breathwork and silence, and beings would speak through them. Individuals did not imagine these conversations. These were supernatural manifestations. And the method was eerily parallel.

I had thought it was divine. But now I had to ask: What if it wasn't?

One example from the episode stuck with me: a possessed individual spoke fluent Latin, mocking the priest, despite having no prior exposure. Another demon revealed personal sins of the deliverance team, intimate things no one else should have known, before being cast out. Not by ritual. Not by energy. They didn't achieve it through good vibes or heightened awareness.

These spirits only responded to one name, Jesus.

Not "Christ consciousness."

Not "universal love."

Not "the divine source."

Only Jesus, the Jesus of Scripture.

That shift in awareness, realizing the power in Jesus' name, forced me to reevaluate everything, including the lives and beliefs of those I had followed so closely.

This realization unraveled everything I thought I knew. But it also opened the door to deeper discernment, and a confrontation with truth I couldn't ignore. And I wasn't alone. As I continued to wrestle with these revelations, I discovered others who had walked a similar path, people who had gone even deeper into the New Age than I had, only to come to the same alarming conclusion.

Many former New Age teachers and mediums have come forward to say the same thing — that what once appeared peaceful and loving was actually a spiritual counterfeit. Angela Maria Scafidi was one of them. She had practiced as a medium, Reiki master, astrologer, and channeled for years. Like many others, she had spiritual encounters that felt divine, even healing. But over time, she noticed a dark presence surrounding her life. She described it as being "spiritually tethered," unable to break free no matter how much light-work she did. Only when she cried out to Jesus did the darkness finally leave her. Angela destroyed all of her occult tools, her tarot cards, crystals, pendulums — and began walking in freedom. She now boldly warns others that many New Age practices are not spiritually neutral; they're gateways to demonic influence.

Another powerful voice is Jenn Nizza. As a professional psychic medium, she thought of her abilities were a gift. She could see and hear spirits, conduct accurate readings, and help people find "closure" with loved ones. But her life became increasingly plagued by oppression. Unseen forces tormented her at night, touching her and creating terrifying presences that haunted her. Eventually, she too cried out to Jesus, and everything changed. Jenn now speaks openly about how the spirits she once welcomed were not deceased loved ones or angels, but demons in disguise. She warns the enemy doesn't mind if you believe in love or light or even "God," as long as it's not the Jesus of the Bible.

Jenn Nizza summarizes time-and-time again that "they" don't care if you call them angels or spirit guides. They just want you as far from Jesus as possible.

Angela Maria Scafidi would state that when she called on Jesus, the spiritual torment stopped. That's when she knew she had been lied to.

Even before I encountered their testimonies, I had noticed cracks, not just in the teachings of New Thought, but in the fruit of the lives behind these people. In interviews and books, these spiritual leaders spoke with flowery language about awakening, peace, and consciousness. But many also endorsed ideologies that clearly stood in opposition to what is good, holy, or true. Some excused sexual immorality. Others blurred the lines between love and lawlessness. Some even mocked biblical values as primitive or regressive. And yet, they claimed to be aligned with angels and light. I couldn't ignore what Jesus said:

"Watch out for false prophets. They come to you in sheep's clothing, but inwardly they are ferocious wolves. By their fruit you will recognize them."
— Matthew 7:15–16

The fruit wasn't righteous. It was thorny, and increasingly rotten. And that realization made one thing clear: Spiritual language does not guarantee spiritual truth.

This confirmed what I was suspecting: not every spirit that offers peace comes from God. In fact, some wear peace like a mask to hide the chains beneath.

Chapter Five: NDEs – Truth, Deception, and Discernment

After realizing not all spirits are good, I had to return to the grounded principles I once knew, truths I had strayed from during my spiritual wanderings. I came back to the Word of God, where evil isn't just symbolic; it's real. And I found Scripture doesn't treat these types of supernatural experiences lightly.

"Let no one be found among you who… practices divination or sorcery, interprets omens, engages in witchcraft, or casts spells, or who is a medium or spiritist… Anyone who does these things is detestable to the Lord."
— Deuteronomy 18:10–12

And here I thought the New Thought I was finding was all new! Like I discovered some sort of emerging unknown gem that gave the answers I was looking for, it was shocking to find out that a book written thousands of years ago spoke directly about this…

It was both humbling and unsettling to realize that what felt like a modern spiritual awakening was, in fact, an ancient deception already warned about in Scripture.

"Once when we were going to the place of prayer, we were met by a female slave who had a spirit by which she predicted the future… She kept this up for many days. Finally Paul became so annoyed that he turned around and said to the spirit, 'In the name of Jesus Christ I command you to come out of her!' At that moment the spirit left her."

— Acts 16:16–18

Even though this girl was proclaiming the truth, identifying Paul as a servant of God, Paul cast the spirit out. Why? Because of its source.

"…He also drove out many demons, but he would not let the demons speak because they knew who he was."

— Mark 1:34

"Demons came out of many people, shouting, 'You are the Son of God!' But he rebuked them and would not allow them to speak…"

— Luke 4:41

Even Jesus silenced demons who acknowledged His identity, because their intent wasn't truth; it was confusion and fear.

Re-Assessing NDE's

There's a common belief in spiritual circles that all NDEs are peaceful encounters with the afterlife, and that no discernment is required. But not all NDEs are the same. After deeply researching and listening to hundreds of accounts, I found a pattern, one that Christians must take seriously.

1. Biblically-Aligned: Heaven NDE's

These are encounters where individuals report:
- Meeting Jesus directly
- A profound awareness of God's holiness
- A sense of judgment and deep repentance
- A mission from God to return and testify

Randy Kay clinically died from a blood clot and stood in the presence of Jesus. He recounts that every question he ever had melted away in the light of Christ's love. Yet, even in that love, the truth of his sin overcame him—not shame, but truth. He knew that this was not some impersonal energy or "source." This was the Lamb of God. He didn't hear, "You're enough," but saw that only Jesus was. When he returned, Randy's life was radically transformed, and he now openly preaches repentance and salvation through Christ alone.

2. Non-Biblical or Deceptive NDE's

These NDEs are the most commonly shared and promoted in mainstream books and videos. They sound positive, sometimes even beautiful, but they subtly preach a gospel without Jesus.

Common themes include:

- "All paths lead to God"
- "There is no hell"
- "You are divine"
- "Your only purpose is self-love and expansion"

These experiences often include beings of light, "higher selves," or energies that communicate love without repentance. The experience accepts everyone; it judges no one.

"But even if we or an angel from heaven should preach a gospel other than the one we preached to you, let them be under God's curse!"

— Galatians 1:8

"The coming of the lawless one… will use all sorts of displays of power through signs and wonders that serve the lie…"

— 2 Thessalonians 2:9–11

They preach peace, but not truth. Light, but not the cross. And that's where we must use discernment.

After studying what Scripture had to say, I knew there had to be an explanation for these contradictions. That's when I came across a category almost no one talks about, a category you'll rarely find in mainstream books or media.

3. Biblically-Aligned: Hell NDE's

These accounts are not abstract; they're vivid, specific, and horrifying. They come from people who were clinically dead or supernaturally shown what lies beyond without Christ. Each testifies of torment, hopelessness, and utter separation from God.

The imagery is often the same:

- Being dragged into darkness
- Demonic beings tormenting the soul
- Screams that never stop
- Flesh burning in an unquenchable fire
- Demons crushing limbs and tearing into flesh
- Maggots eating their flesh as they lay there helplessly

These are not metaphors, they are recurring testimonies from across cultures and backgrounds.

But among these, there is a specific pattern that adds another layer of urgency: the deception that precedes the descent.

Some of these individuals did not fall straight into Hell; something led them there. Initially, the being who appeared to them seemed kind, peaceful, and even divine. The environment felt tranquil. The presence seemed radiant. But as the experience deepened, that peace gave way to confusion… then terror… then torment.

What once felt safe felt strange. Darkness fell. The guide's demeanor shifted, subtle at first, then unmistakable. The warmth faded into cold indifference. Reassurance gave way to dread. And eventually, the being revealed its true nature, dragging the person into darkness.

These stories show that evil does not always present itself as evil. Sometimes it wears the face of comfort.

Buddhist tradition shaped Steve Kang's upbringing in South Korea, after which he immigrated to the United States. After battling addiction and severe depression, he began hearing a voice that claimed to be his deceased grandfather. The voice was soothing, even spiritual. It promised peace, but only through death.

Under its influence, Steve took a deadly combination of drugs and then slit both his throat and abdomen. As he bled out on the floor, he expected release. Instead, he fell into darkness, literally.

In his testimony, Steve described being dragged into hell. He said, "The heat intensified. I heard screaming all around me. I could feel pain. I realized this wasn't a dream, I was dead and in Hell." He saw demonic creatures — vile, humanoid beings that clawed at him, laughed at his torment, and fed on his fear.

Steve cried out for help, but no one came. Miraculously, he survived his physical injuries, and the hospital revived him. Upon awakening, he felt both gratitude and terror.

He later came to faith in Jesus Christ, recognizing that the voice he had followed was not his grandfather but a deceiving spirit.

Howard Storm, a professor of art and a staunch atheist, collapsed from a sudden illness while visiting Paris in 1985. His stomach had ruptured, and doctors gave him little chance of survival. As he slipped into unconsciousness, his spirit separated from his body.

He first found himself in a dim hospital room, hearing voices calling him from the hallway. The beings that appeared looked human and friendly, but the farther he followed them into the dark, the more sinister they became.

Eventually, they turned on him. In an abyss of terror, these creatures violently attacked, scratched, bit, and tore at Howard. He described the experience as being utterly devoid of hope. He realized: "This is Hell. I'm in Hell."

In his desperation, he remembered Jesus, not from belief, but from a childhood memory. He cried out, "Jesus, save me!" And immediately, the light of Christ appeared. The demonic beings fled. Christ rescued, healed, and showed Howard a vision of his life.

He later gave his life to Christ and became a pastor. His book, *My Descent Into Death*, details his experience.

In each account, those who escaped did so only by crying out to Jesus. By means other than willpower. Not by light or vibration. Not by being a good person.

What would have happened if they hadn't come back to life?

"Just as people are destined to die once, and after that to face judgment…"
— *Hebrews 9:27*

Their return was not their reward; it was God's mercy. God spared them from eternity. But many do not return.

These stories are disturbing, but they are also merciful warnings.

If deception is possible in this world, through false spirits and teachings, then we must also be discerning about spiritual experiences, especially those that happen at the threshold of life and death.

"Dear friends, do not believe every spirit, but test the spirits to see whether they are from God, because many false prophets have gone out into the world."
—1 John 4:1

The deception is not that hell doesn't exist. The deception is that you won't end up there.

This is fundamental to Satan's plan: the distortion of truth, not the outright denial of God, five truths and one lie. There's no need to erase belief in the divine; just deny Jesus, God in the flesh. You can believe in love, light, healing, energy, even angels, as long as you deny the one name that has power over him. The only name that saves.

"For God so loved the world that he gave his one and only Son, that whoever believes in him shall not perish but have eternal life."
— John 3:16

"If you declare with your mouth, 'Jesus is Lord,' and believe in your heart that God raised him from the dead, you will be saved."
— Romans 10:9

In the next chapter, we'll inspect one of the most eye-opening NDEs I've ever come across, the testimony of Howard Pittman. His story is not just a glimpse into the afterlife, but a direct confrontation with deception itself. And unlike many vague or symbolic accounts, his encounter pulls back the curtain with crystal clarity.

Chapter 6: Howard Pittman's NDE

The Devil's Kingdom, and the Deception of the Lukewarm Church

As we discussed, not every near-death experience leads to flowers and angels.

Some peel back a reality far more urgent, one that forces you to reckon with the war for your soul, the schemes of Satan, and the tragic state of the modern church. That was Howard Pittman's experience.

He was a Baptist preacher. A man who believed he had done the Lord's work. But on August 3, 1979, after suffering a massive aortic rupture, Pittman's spirit left his body and stepped into the unseen realm.

And what he encountered was not what he had expected.

The Devil's Whisper: "Submit Your Spirit to Me"

The first voice Pittman heard after death was not God's.

It was the devil.

But it didn't sound dark or threatening. It was smooth, kind, and pleasing. The voice called to him gently, even with what felt like authority. There was no smell of sulfur. No frightful appearance. If anything, it felt... holy.

The voice told Pittman to submit his spirit, to hand over his breath.

For a moment, he considered it. After all, wasn't this the afterlife? Wasn't this voice holy? It seemed to carry a weight, almost like that of an angel. There was no reason on the surface to doubt its legitimacy. The tone was reverent. The presence was powerful. The setting felt right.

But something deep within resisted. A flicker of discernment, a whisper of truth stronger than the seduction, rose within him. With the last ounce of free will he had left, Pittman refused.

That choice mattered more than he realized. It wasn't just a metaphor. It was a test. A genuine attempt by the enemy to claim a soul under the pretense of light.

And it *almost* worked.

"For false messiahs and false prophets will appear and perform great signs and wonders to deceive, if possible, even the elect."
— *Matthew 24:24*

This was deception at its most dangerous: not evil masquerading as evil, but evil masquerading as divine.

Before the Throne: A Crushing Realization

After refusing the devil, angels appeared and escorted him to what he understood to be the gates of the Kingdom. There, God Himself granted Pittman the unspeakable privilege of presenting a plea.

He thought it would be simple.

He had been a pastor.

He had shared the gospel.

Surely, his works would count for something.

But then the voice of God thundered, a voice that sounded like many rushing waters, and it shattered him.

God told him that his life had been a failure.

Not because he hadn't done good things, but because he had done them for **S E L F.**

He had professed God with his mouth, but his heart was far from Him. He had been a "mouth professor," not a "heart possessor." God showed him that the stains on his garments were his good deeds, done in pride, not surrender.

"Not everyone who says to me, 'Lord, Lord,' will enter the kingdom of heaven, but only the one who does the will of my Father."
— Matthew 7:21

In that moment, Pittman realized the difference between serving God and having a genuine relationship with God. It was a terrifying revelation, and one that many in the modern church still need to hear.

He pleaded for his life, not for himself, but for the sake of delivering a message. God, in His grace, sent him back.

But first, he saw something even more disturbing.

Through the Kingdom of Darkness

Before returning to his body, the angels took Pittman on a guided tour of Satan's kingdom.

What he saw was structured, efficient, and militaristic. Not chaos. Not random evil. A government.

Demons were not roaming aimlessly; they were ranked, each with assignments and authority based on their position. Here are some classifications he witnessed:

1. Principalities of Nations

These demons had oversight over entire countries. They influenced governments, stirred wars, and deceived populations through ideologies, false religions, and counterfeit peace movements.

2. Powers of Religion

These were not demons of atheism, but of false religion. They inspired works-based belief systems, counterfeit "revivals," and even infiltrated churches with doctrines that diminished the authority of Jesus or elevated man's experience above truth.

3. Rulers of the Darkness

These demons specialized in twisting truth into half-truths. They confused moral lines, promoted spiritual compromise, and seeded false light, New Age teachings, "spirit guides," and any movement that removed the cross while still sounding spiritual.

4. Spirits of Addiction and Bondage

Assigned to individuals and bloodlines, these demons created strongholds, lust, addiction, pride, greed, envy, hatred, and were activated by legal rights: sin, generational curses, or unrepented doorways.

5. Demons Assigned to Churches

This was perhaps the most shocking. Pittman saw demons assigned specifically to Christian congregations, especially in the West. They whispered pride into pulpits, hardened hearts in pews, and made churches lukewarm, more focused on comfort, growth, and self-image than repentance, holiness, or the Lordship of Christ.

It was the perfect plan: don't remove God, just dilute Him. Don't destroy the Church, just sedate it.

"You say, 'I am rich; I have acquired wealth and do not need a thing.' But you do not realize that you are wretched, pitiful, poor, blind and naked."
— *Revelation 3:17*

The Message: The Church Must Wake Up

God allowed Pittman to return, but with one mission:

Warn the Church.

He was to tell them that Satan's kingdom is real, organized, and active. That the Church is, by and large, asleep. That many who claim to serve God are merely wearing religious masks, unaware they are spiritually dead inside.

He saw that Satan's dominant strategy wasn't to oppose the Church; it was to join it. To preach from its pulpits. To influence its theology. To lull it into lukewarmness.

And the greatest deception of all? That you can "believe" in God, serve Him publicly, and yet never actually know Him.

"I know your deeds, that you are neither cold nor hot. I wish you were either one or the other! So, because you

are lukewarm... I am about to spit you out of my

mouth."

— *Revelation 3:15–16*

Final Reflection

Pittman's story is not a sensational tale, it's a sobering warning.

This war is real. The devil is real. But more real still is the authority of Jesus Christ, who gives power to the truly surrendered, those who are not just mouth professors, but heart possessors.

The light you walk in, make sure it is not a lie.

Howard Pittman's Key Takeaways to the Church

1. Satan's Kingdom Is Real and Organized

The devil doesn't operate through chaos. He rules through structure. He ranks his demonic forces like a military, each with specific assignments to deceive, distract, and destroy. Many Christians underestimate his intelligence and strategies.

2. False Light Is the Most Dangerous Lie

Not everything that feels good is from God. The enemy presents himself as an angel of light, mimicking the voice of God and flattering the ego. If you don't know the real thing, the counterfeit will feel authentic.

3. Many Churches Are Lukewarm

Pittman saw firsthand that many congregations had faced infiltration. The sermons were powerless; the people were spiritually asleep, and the focus was on comfort, not conviction. These churches were on autopilot, unaware they were being subtly seduced.

4. Many Christians Are "Mouth Professors" Not "Heart Possessors"

Professing faith means nothing if your heart doesn't belong to Christ. Until God revealed that his works were self-serving, Pittman believed he was a good Christian. This warning is clear: religious activity without surrender is deception.

This has nothing to do with earning salvation through works. Scripture is clear:

"It is by grace you have been saved, through faith...
not by works, so that no one can boast."
— Ephesians 2:8–9

The issue isn't how much you do for God; it's whether you truly know Him. Being a heart possessor means you've actually submitted your life to Christ in faith. It's not about perfection; it's about possession.

"If anyone does not have the Spirit of Christ, they do
not belong to Christ."
— Romans 8:9

Genuine faith always results in surrender. Not to earn love, but because you've received it.

5. The Church Must Wake Up, Now

This is not the time for spiritual laziness or casual faith. God allowed Pittman to return for one reason: to warn us. The Church must return to repentance, intimacy with Jesus, and full-hearted obedience. Anything less is open ground for the enemy.

Howard's story was a wake-up call, not just about the existence of evil, but about the urgency of salvation. Which leads to the next question: What does it actually mean to be saved?

Chapter 7: Diminishing Christ – How Islam Rewrites Jesus in the Name of God

Satan rarely begins with outright denial. That's too obvious. Instead, he wraps the lie in light, smoothing it over with familiar truth until it feels warm, safe, even divine. He doesn't remove Jesus. He rebrands Him.

That's why Satan's most effective tactic isn't to deny Christ's existence, but to diminish His identity.

Just enough truth to be convincing.
Just enough distortion to cost eternity.

Islam is one of the clearest examples of this. It gets so much right, enough to fool the undiscerning, enough to draw admiration from the spiritually curious.

A Faith Built on Reverence — and Redefinition

Islam reveres Jesus (or "Isa") as a great prophet, born of a virgin, who performed miracles, and who will even return again.

That's the "five" truths already.

And here's the sixth:

Islam is radically monotheistic. "There is no god but Allah." This command echoes the Shema of Israel and would seem to honor the God of Abraham.

But it's the one lie, carefully buried beneath those truths, that changes everything:

Jesus is not the Son of God.

Jesus was not crucified.

Jesus is not divine.

Jesus is not the Savior.

The Deception Begins: A Cave and an Angel

Roughly 600 years after Jesus died and rose again, a man named Muhammad went into a cave outside Mecca to meditate. He was seeking spiritual truth in a world filled with paganism and tribal violence. There, in the Cave of Hira, he claimed to be visited by an angel, who forcefully commanded him to "Read!" or "Recite!" even though Muhammad was illiterate.

The being identified itself as the angel Gabriel, and this encounter marked the beginning of the revelations that would become the Qur'an.

Muhammad was so shaken by the experience that he thought he might be possessed by a demon. He even considered taking his own life. But his wife, Khadijah, and her cousin Waraqah, convinced him the angel was from God.

From that moment, Muhammad believed God chose him to restore Abraham's one true religion. And with that, a new religion was born, one that honored Jesus, but rewrote Him.

What began in a cave would soon spread across nations. But the message it carried, though cloaked in truth, carried a devastating distortion.

Could it be that Muhammad truly encountered something supernatural in the cave of Hira? Could it be that the being who revealed the Qur'an was indeed an angelic presence, genuinely divine in appearance, and unquestionably powerful? Perhaps Muhammad's initial fears of demonic possession were right after all, but tragically dismissed. For even Satan himself masquerades as an angel of light (2 Corinthians 11:14).

"But even if we or an angel from heaven should preach a gospel other than the one we preached to you, let them be under God's curse"

— Galatians 1:8

I believe this wasn't simply a human invention. The power, the influence, and the profound reverence Islam inspires are undeniably supernatural, but they're not from the true God. They're part of a deeper deception, orchestrated by Satan himself to pull humanity away from the real Jesus and the saving truth of His cross. The enemy's greatest triumph isn't to deny spiritual encounters altogether; it's mimicking them, to distort them just enough to deceive, confuse, and mislead those earnestly seeking God.

The Most Strategic Lie: A Hollow Christ

The Qur'an acknowledges Jesus' existence, but strategically hollows Him out. It removes His power, denies His sacrifice, and replaces His glory with a role that Satan can control: a noble man, but not the Son of the Living God.

The truth is this: Satan doesn't mind if you believe in Jesus, as long as it's not the real Jesus.

Islam's version of Jesus is stripped of His deity, stripped of the cross, and turned into a forerunner for someone else, Muhammad, whom the Qur'an presents as the final and greatest prophet. And with that, Satan has redirected the world's largest religious population away from the One who actually saves.

It's a spiritual sleight of hand, and it works.

A Gospel Without a Cross Is No Gospel At All

In Islam, no one crucified Jesus. Surah 4:157 says they only made it appear so. Someone else — perhaps Judas, some claim — was made to look like Jesus and was crucified in His place.

But if there was no cross, there was no atonement. If there was no sacrifice, there is no salvation. And if Jesus didn't die, then He never rose. The entire gospel collapses under that single lie.

> "Without the shedding of blood there is no forgiveness."
> — Hebrews 9:22

Islam offers a Jesus without the blood, a God without the Son, and a faith without the Savior.

The Antichrist Pattern: Deny the Son, Keep the Language of Light

Scripture warns us plainly:

> *"Who is the liar? It is whoever denies that Jesus is the Christ. Such a person is the antichrist—denying the Father and the Son."*
> — *1 John 2:22*

And again:

"Every spirit that does not acknowledge Jesus is not from God. This is the spirit of the antichrist."
— *1 John 4:3*

The antichrist spirit doesn't always come with horns. Sometimes it comes cloaked in tradition, morality, and reverent language about God.

But the litmus test is always the same: What do they say about Jesus?

Islam speaks of Him, yes.

But it does not exalt Him.

It does not glorify the cross.

It does not declare Him Lord.

That's the lie within the light.

The Final Blow: No Need for a Savior If There's No Sin

Another subtle twist: in Islam, salvation isn't through Christ; it's through works.

- Pray five times daily.
- Fast during Ramadan.
- Go to Mecca.
- Be good.
- Hope your good outweighs your bad.

The system itself seems pious until you realize it nullifies the need for a Savior. And that's exactly what Satan wants: a world trying harder instead of surrendering to Christ.

Foundations of Islam

Now let's summarize the foundations of Islam to understand how the lie developed. It helps to see the framework Satan used to mirror biblical truth while subtly dismantling Christ's centrality.

Element	Detail
Claim of Apostacy	Muhammad claimed Jews and Christians had corrupted the original faith of Abraham. Islam teaches that the original monotheistic religion (Islam) was practiced by prophets like Abraham and Moses but became distorted over time. To them, Christians misrepresented Jesus as divine. Muhammad was sent to restore the original message.
Angel Visit	Angel Gabriel appeared to Muhammad, delivering revelations from God (Allah). These revelations continued over 23 years and became the Qur'an.
New Revelation	The Qur'an was dictated to Muhammad as the final revelation of God. Muslims believe the Qur'an is the literal, unaltered word of Allah, revealed in Arabic. It is considered the final scripture, superseding the Bible, which they claim was altered.
Restoration Message	Islam was framed as a restoration of the pure monotheistic faith of Abraham. Islam positions itself as restoring the faith of Abraham (Ibrahim), focusing on strict monotheism (tawhid) and rejecting Trinitarian doctrine.
One True Faith	Islam teaches it is the final, complete, and correct faith. The

Element	Detail
	Qur'an states that Islam is the religion approved by Allah (Surah 3:19). All other religious expressions are seen as incomplete or invalid.
False Prophet-Leader	Muhammad was illiterate but revered as the Seal of the Prophets. Muhammad's inability to read or write is viewed as evidence that the Qur'an was not his own invention. He is called the last prophet (khatam an-nabiyyin), closing the line of revelation.
Scripture Outside the Bible	Qur'an and Hadiths (sayings and acts of Muhammad). In addition to the Qur'an, Muslims rely on Hadith collections for guidance in daily life, law, and interpretation. These are attributed to eyewitnesses of Muhammad's words and actions.

The Question of Final Authority

This is where the question becomes unavoidable.

Whose voice do we trust? Are we to consume the Word already given, the one that was made flesh, that dwelt among us, that fulfilled the Law, tore the veil, and ushered in a new covenant of grace, spirit, and salvation? Or are we to place our faith in something newly written, a word that not only adds to, but ultimately replaces the very gift God sealed through the death and resurrection of His Son?

It's not just about which scripture is older, or which prophet claimed what. It's about which covenant God has declared as finished.

To accept a new revelation that subverts the gospel is to say:

Insufficient was the veil being torn. The cross was not enough. The Son was not enough.

But Scripture warns us:

"I warn everyone who hears the words of the prophecy of this scroll: If anyone adds anything to them, God will add to that person the plagues described in this scroll. And if anyone takes words away from this scroll of prophecy, God will take away from that

person any share in the tree of life and in the Holy

City, which are described in this scroll."

— Revelation 22:18–19

This isn't a minor issue.

This is a matter of eternity.

Two Saviors: One Real, One Reversed

Here's the chilling part.

The one Islam waits for is the very one the Bible warns about.

Islam teaches Jesus will return, but not to reign as Lord and Savior. Instead, he will come back to:

- Break all crosses (symbolically denying His crucifixion),
- Deny the Trinity, and

- Support the coming of another figure known as the Mahdi.

This Mahdi is Islam's final deliverer, a political, military, and spiritual leader who will establish global Islam and bring justice.

And here's where the inversion happens: The Islamic savior sounds eerily like the Christian Antichrist. And the Islamic version of Jesus supports him.

The Parallels Are Too Precise to Ignore

From a biblical prophetic lens, here's what Scripture says the Antichrist will do:

Biblical Prophecy	Description of Antichrist
Global Political Leader (Revelation 13:7)	Given authority over every tribe, people, language, and nation.
Performs Miraculous	Uses counterfeit signs and wonders to deceive the world.

Biblical Prophecy	Description of Antichrist
Signs (2 Thess. 2:9, Rev. 13:13)	
Brings a False Peace (Daniel 9:27, 1 Thess. 5:3)	Makes a covenant of peace that is later broken. People proclaim peace and safety but sudden destruction comes.
Denies the Father and the Son (1 John 2:22)	Attacks the true identity of Jesus, the Holy Spirit, and the nature of God.
Opposes and Replaces True Worship (2 Thess. 2:4)	Exalts himself above all that is called God and sets himself up in God's temple, proclaiming to be God.
Demands Global Allegiance (Revelation 13:4, 15-17)	Causes all to receive a mark to buy or sell establishing a one-world system.

Now compare that to Islamic eschatology:

Islamic Prophecy	Role of the Mahdi
Global Leader	Unites Muslims and leads the world under Islamic law.

Islamic Prophecy	Role of the Mahdi
Supported by Miracles	Accompanied by the Islamic Jesus, who performs signs.
Brings Peace	Establishes justice and peace after military conquest.
Destroys Crosses	Symbolically rejects Jesus' crucifixion.
Denies the Trinity	Affirms strict monotheism (tawhid), rejecting Father, Son, and the Holy Spirit.
Implements Worldwide Sharia	All are called to submit to Islamic rules by persuasion or force.

The convergence is unmistakable. The Christian Antichrist and the Islamic Mahdi share the same attributes, but from opposing sides.

Islam hails as the redeemer what Christians view as the ultimate deceiver. What Christians call apostasy, Islam calls revelation. What Christians call the real Jesus, Islam enlists as the Mahdi's assistant, denying the very mission He came to fulfill.

This is not a coincidence. This is Satan's masterpiece…

- A false messiah,
- Backed by a rebranded Jesus,
- Introducing a global counterfeit kingdom,
- All while using the language of peace, justice, and God.

This is how Satan works: not by creating a blatant evil, but by mirroring the truth in reverse.

If you are not familiar with the real Jesus — crucified, risen, and reigning — you will end up following a version of Him that leads straight into darkness.

A Hopeful Awakening: How Jesus Is Reaching The Muslim World

But here's the beautiful part of the story.

Satan may craft lies in the shadows, but he cannot stop the light.

In the very regions where the true gospel is forbidden, and people destroy churches and Bibles are illegal, Jesus continues to appear, not through systems or pulpits, but in dreams and visions beyond anyone's silencing.

In countless Muslim nations, especially in the Middle East, North Africa, and parts of Asia, there is a quiet spiritual revolution underway. It's called the underground church.

Nothing physical makes up these churches. Living stones — men and women who risk everything to follow the true Jesus — make up these churches. Many of them have never seen a Bible in their native language. Others meet in whispered prayer behind closed doors, knowing that discovery could mean imprisonment or death.

And yet... they are growing faster than almost anywhere else in the world.

Jesus Is Appearing to Them — Literally

One of the most stunning and well-documented phenomena of our time is this:

Jesus is appearing to Muslims in their dreams.

These are not subtle feelings or abstract thoughts. These are vivid, transformative encounters, where Jesus comes clothed in white, full of light, speaking their language, calling them by name, and revealing Himself as the Son of God.

And the result? Conversion. Repentance. Surrender. Boldness.

Former Muslims, who are now some of the most courageous Christians alive today, encountered Jesus supernaturally, often in the very places where He is not permitted.

Here are just a few patterns being observed:

- People who've never heard the gospel wake up from a dream saying, "I met a man named Jesus. Who is He?"
- Refugees and displaced people groups encounter Christ during their greatest moments of trauma and desperation.
- Entire households are coming to faith after one person has a dream and boldly shares what they've seen.
- Former imams, warlords, and even persecutors of Christians are repenting and becoming evangelists.

It's happening in Iran, in Afghanistan, in Saudi Arabia, in Somalia, and beyond. Often, these are places where no missionary can legally enter, and yet… Christ enters, anyway.

He is not bound by borders. Not limited by politics. Not silenced by laws.

The same Jesus who appeared to Saul on the road to Damascus is still appearing today, on dusty floors in Syrian villages, in urban slums of Cairo, in locked bedrooms of hijab-covered women crying out to God in the night.

The Unstoppable Gospel

The enemy's lie may seem strong, but the gospel is stronger.

"I will build my church, and the gates of hell will not prevail against it."
— Matthew 16:18

For every counterfeit Christ, there is the true Christ calling people's home. For every system of works, there is the gift of grace freely offered. And for every shadow of deception, there is the piercing light of truth.

So yes, Islam, like many systems, has been used to diminish Jesus. But Jesus is not finished. He's not silent. And He's not waiting for permission.

He's coming in dreams.

He's speaking in visions.

He's igniting courage in the hearts of believers.

And He's breaking into the last places on earth Satan thought he had locked down.

The gospel is not fragile. It's not failing. It's not falling behind.

It is moving, multiplying, and miraculously transforming lives in the exact places darkness hoped to reign forever.

Chapter 8: Wolves in Sheep's Clothing, False Prophets

There's a growing trend that feels right, but isn't. It looks like light. It sounds like truth. But if you trace it back, not to your feelings, not to culture, but to Scripture, you'll find a deadly distortion hiding in plain sight.

This chapter isn't about throwing stones. It's about sounding the alarm.

Jesus warned us clearly:

> *"Watch out for false prophets. They come to you in sheep's clothing, but inwardly they are ferocious wolves."*
>
> — *Matthew 7:15 (NIV)*

Wolves don't announce themselves. They sneak in. They blend. And they often use just enough truth to sell a lie.

Patterns of Deception

The deception we see today isn't new; it's recycled. In fact, you'll notice the same spiritual patterns repeating themselves across New Age teachings, New Thought movements, and even Islam: a promise of hidden knowledge, a centering of self, and a distancing from the biblical Jesus.

But perhaps most disturbing is how these same patterns are creeping into churches. Not all at once. Not through loud proclamations. But slowly, subtly, through teaching that tickles ears but starves souls.

A Gospel of Comfort, Not Conversion

Modern false teachings don't always deny God. They dilute Him. While promising peace, they eliminate repentance. The teachings offer grace without transformation and favor without faithfulness.

One example is the prosperity gospel, which suggests that God's favor is measured by financial success. Another example is the downplaying of sin, where people label conviction as shame, and view repentance as outdated. And perhaps the most seductive of all: a gospel that elevates self above submission.

But the Bible makes it clear:

"There will be false teachers among you. They will secretly introduce destructive heresies... Many will follow their depraved conduct and will bring the way of truth into disrepute."
— 2 Peter 2:1–2

If sin doesn't matter, then the cross doesn't matter. And if the cross doesn't matter, we are still dead in our sins.

The enemy doesn't always tempt with rebellion. Sometimes he tempts with affirmation, "You are enough," "Follow your heart," "Your truth is truth." But Scripture tells a different story:

"The heart is deceitful above all things and beyond cure. Who can understand it?"
— Jeremiah 17:9

"Trust in the Lord with all your heart and lean not on your own understanding."
— Proverbs 3:5

The Great Counterfeit: The Gospel of Self

Teachings from Tomi Arayomi, whose clear articulation of how self-worship subtly replaces Christ-centered surrender significantly influenced the insights in the following section, shaped my understanding of this spiritual deception. While all truth ultimately belongs to God, I gratefully acknowledge Tomi Arayomi's faithful work in highlighting the following critical message.

We are now living in a time when the most culturally accepted form of worship is self-worship. This "gospel of self" dresses itself in emotional healing, empowerment, and even pseudo-Christian vocabulary. But at its core, it replaces Christ with the self as center.

We have made self-love the new altar, sacrificing God for the illusion of personal peace. This is one of the first signs we are living in perilous times, not because loving yourself in a healthy, God-given identity is wrong, but because this movement teaches us to elevate self above God, to deify our desires, and to dismantle anything, truth included, that stands in the way of our comfort.

What caused Lucifer to fall wasn't hatred toward God; it was an obsession with himself. He exalted his own throne, his own will, and his own image. That same spirit now whispers into today's culture: "Put yourself first. You are the light. You are divine." And in doing so, people unknowingly trade surrender for self-exaltation.

"How you have fallen from heaven, morning star, son of the dawn! You have been cast down to the earth, you who once laid low the nations! You said in your heart, 'I will ascend to the heavens; I will raise my throne above the stars of God; I will sit enthroned on the mount of assembly, on the utmost heights of Mount Zaphon. I will ascend above the tops of the clouds; I will make myself like the Most High.'"
— *Isaiah 14:12-14*

"Your heart became proud on account of your beauty, and you corrupted your wisdom because of your splendor. So I threw you to the earth; I made a spectacle of you before kings."
— *Ezekiel 28:17*

People who constantly focus on themselves often suffer the most. They become anxious not because life is uncertain, but because they're carrying the weight of their own godhood. When you are the center of your own universe, anxiety becomes inevitable, because deep down, you know you can't save yourself. You are not strong enough to carry your sin, your shame, or your suffering. But the self-love gospel keeps pushing this burden as if it's a badge of honor.

This gospel is a counterfeit, not because it doesn't offer peace, but because it places peace above truth. Instruction in self-love precedes an understanding of love. It teaches healing without holiness. It teaches identity without repentance. And worst of all, it puts you on the throne while pushing Jesus to the periphery.

When Self Becomes God

People deeply entrenched in self-love theology are often the hardest to reach. Why? Because they look godly. Scripture may be quoted by them. They might be spiritual. They might even serve in ministry. But underneath the surface, they've turned themselves into their own saviors. They've become their own god.

This makes the dangerous, not in the sense that they intend harm, but because they dismantle truth for peace. They silence conviction for the sake of comfort. They reshape doctrine to accommodate trauma rather than letting the true Healer bring redemption.

These individuals often possess just enough Scripture to sound convincing, but not enough surrender to be transformed. And they often carry just enough trauma to be untouchable, hiding behind pain as a shield against truth. Pain becomes the lens through which they interpret God, rather than letting God heal the pain.

"People will be lovers of themselves, lovers of money, boastful, proud, abusive... having a form of godliness

but denying its power. Have nothing to do with such

people."

— 2 Timothy 3:2–5

Self-love without surrender is not love; it's idolatry.

And when people place themselves at the center, they become unreachable, not because God cannot reach them, but because they've stopped listening. They've become wise in their own eyes. And when you're your own god, there's no room for the real one.

Dismantling Truth for Comfort

Many of these movements disguise themselves as inclusive and compassionate. But the cost of that compassion is often truth itself. We see pastors refusing to preach on sin, churches more concerned with branding than the Bible, and messages that comfort the sinner rather than convict the soul.

This is not love. This is deception. It is the serpent's whisper repackaged: "Did God really say…?"

> *"Woe to those who call evil good and good evil, who put darkness for light and light for darkness."*
> — *Isaiah 5:20 (NIV)*

The result? A seemingly vibrant church is, in reality, spiritually dormant. A faith-empowering church that lacks power. The creation of a generation that knows of God, but doesn't walk with Him.

How Do We Discern?

- Know the Word. If you don't know the truth, you can't recognize a lie.
- Test the fruit. A teaching that leads you closer to self and farther from surrender is not of God.
- Stay humble. Pride is the soil where deception grows.

- Remain in Christ. The closer you walk with Jesus, the easier it is to see what doesn't align.

"Finally, be strong in the Lord and in his mighty power. Put on the full armor of God, so that you can take your stand against the devil's schemes."

"For our struggle is not against flesh and blood, but against the rulers, against the authorities, against the powers of this dark world and against the spiritual forces of evil in the heavenly realms."

"Therefore put on the full armor of God, so that when the day of evil comes, you may be able to stand your ground... Stand firm then, with the belt of truth buckled around your waist, with the breastplate of righteousness in place, and with your feet fitted with the readiness that comes from the gospel of peace... Take up the shield of faith... the helmet of salvation

and the sword of the Spirit, which is the word of

God."

— Ephesians 6:10–18 (selected, NIV)

Final Thought

We are not at war with people, we are at war with deception. And the most dangerous lies are the ones that feel true. That sound spiritual. That look holy.

But if Jesus is not at the center, truly at the center, it is not the gospel. This is the dividing line, the absolute claim that stands above every counterfeit:

"I am the way and the truth and the life. No one comes to the Father except through me."

— John 14:6 (NIV)

The sheep will know the Shepherd's voice. But first, we must learn to listen.

Chapter 9: What It Means to Be Saved

The Fulfillment of the Covenant and the Call to Surrender

You can't talk about light without talking about Jesus. You can't talk about truth, salvation, or eternity without passing through one narrow gate: Him.

Jesus isn't one option among many. He isn't a prophet pointing to truth, He is the Truth. And until you understand why He had to come, you'll never understand what it means to be saved.

The Old Covenant: Law and Justice

In the Old Testament, God gave the Israelites a covenant. It was based on law, commands, sacrifices, and obedience. It revealed God's holiness and justice, but also our problem: we can't keep it.

The law wasn't the problem; we were.

"Therefore no one will be declared righteous in God's sight by the works of the law; rather, through the law we become conscious of our sin."

— *Romans 3:20*

The law was a mirror. It showed us who we really were: guilty. And in God's system of justice, sin demands a penalty, and that penalty is death.

"The wages of sin is death…"

— *Romans 6:23*

That's not just physical death, it's spiritual separation from God. Under the old covenant, animal sacrifices were made as temporary coverings for sin. But none of it could actually take sin away. It just pointed forward to the only One who could.

The Fulfillment: Jesus Didn't Abolish the Law — He Completed It

Jesus came not to replace the law, but to <u>fulfill</u> it.

"Do not think that I have come to abolish the Law or the Prophets; I have not come to abolish them but to fulfill them."
— Matthew 5:17

He lived the perfect life we couldn't. He obeyed every command, never sinned, and then died as the final sacrifice. The innocent for the guilty. The righteous for the rebellious.

And because of that, the covenant changed. <u>The veil tore</u>. The covenant paid the penalty.

We are no longer saved by law, but by grace.

As Paul emphasized in his letter to the Ephesians:

"For it is by grace you have been saved, through faith—and this is not from yourselves, it is the gift of God—not by works, so that no one can boast."
— *Ephesians 2:8–9*

Ray Comfort and the Use of the Law

People know Evangelist Ray Comfort for asking a simple question: "Have you ever told a lie?"

What he's doing is using the law the way Jesus did, not as a ladder to climb, but a light to expose. He walks through the Ten Commandments not to shame people, but to show them the truth: we're no good.

Have you lied? Stolen? Looked with lust? Used God's name casually?

That's all sin.

And Ray doesn't just stop at the surface; he presses deeper: "If you've stolen anything, what does that make you?" A thief. "If you've told a lie, what does that make you?" A liar. "If you've looked with lust, Jesus says you've already committed adultery in your heart." By that standard, we're not just people who "make mistakes"; we're lying, thieving, blasphemous adulterers at heart.

Ray's approach makes it clear: if God is good, He must punish sin. And if we stand before Him on judgment day without a Savior, we'll get justice, not mercy.

But he doesn't stop there. He points to the cross, and this is where the courtroom analogy goes even deeper.

It's as if you're standing before the Judge, fully guilty. No excuses. No loopholes. The gavel is about to come down. But then, Jesus walks in, not to argue your case, but to pay your fine.

Not with silver. Not with an animal sacrifice. But with Himself.

"The next day John saw Jesus coming toward him and said, 'Look, the Lamb of God, who takes away the sin of the world!'"
— John 1:29

On the cross, Jesus absorbed the penalty that we owed. He paid it in full. His last words weren't "Try harder" or "You still owe", they were:

"It is finished."
— John 19:30

In Greek, that phrase is tetelestai—a legal term stamped on ancient debts. It means: paid in full.

God, in His love, stepped into our courtroom. Jesus took our punishment, not so we could live however we want, but so we could be reconciled. So, we could repent and believe and live from a new heart.

That's what it means to be saved.

What Salvation Is (and Isn't)

Salvation is not:

- Saying a quick prayer because you're afraid of hell
- Trying to be a "good person" and hoping it's enough
- Getting baptized without repentance
- Attending church and checking the box

Salvation is:

- Realizing you are guilty before a holy God
- Believing Jesus paid your debt in full
- Turning away from sin (repentance)
- Trusting in Christ alone for salvation
- Entering a genuine relationship with Him

It is simple, but not shallow.

This is not narrow-minded; it's narrow by design. Jesus is the only way, because only Jesus dealt with sin.

Grace Is Not Permission—It's Power

Many people misunderstand grace. They think it means God overlooks sin. But grace isn't a pass. It's power to walk in the new life.

"What shall we say, then? Shall we go on sinning so that grace may increase? By no means!"
— Romans 6:1–2

When you're saved, you're not just forgiven; you're transformed. The Spirit of God fills you, and your desires begin to change. You now have a new heart that wants to follow Him.

This doesn't mean perfection. It means direction. Your life turns toward Christ. Your heart bends toward obedience, not out of fear, but out of love.

So… Are You Saved?

Not, "Did you grow up in church?"

Not, "Did you ask Jesus into your heart one time?"

But are you born again?

Do you actually know Him?

Has your heart been changed?

"Examine yourselves to see whether you are in the faith; test yourselves. Do you not realize that Christ Jesus is in you—unless, of course, you fail the test?"
— 2 Corinthians 13:5

The greatest tragedy isn't living an awful life.

It's living a decent life, while never being saved.

Closing Call

You can't earn your way in. You can't "positive energy" your way through. Christian language and good intentions do not provide a shield.

You must be born again.

You must repent and believe.

You must come to the cross, not with your resume, but with surrender.

The price was <u>paid.</u>

But you must still receive it.

Chapter 10: Answering the "What Now?" (Our Calling)

An important figure in my life once asked me a question that's lingered in my heart ever since: "If we're saved by faith, then other than being saved... what's the point? What are we supposed to do about it? Is this life just something to endure until heaven?"

That question struck me deeply. It pierced through all the theological clutter and landed right at the feet of our purpose.

Because it's true, if salvation is the end of the story, then why are we still here?

But Scripture tells us that salvation is just the beginning.

From Encounter to Mission

To answer the "what now," we don't need to look any further than the story of Paul, originally known as Saul of Tarsus. Saul was an educated man with Roman citizenship, trained under the best teachers of Jewish law. He had influence, status, and comfort. He was zealous for religion, and believed he was doing God's will by persecuting the early Christians.

He approved of the stoning of Stephen, the first Christian martyr, and actively sought to imprison and silence followers of Jesus. Until the day he encountered the risen Christ.

While traveling to Damascus to arrest more believers, a blinding light from heaven knocked him to the ground, and he heard a voice:

> *"Saul, Saul, why do you persecute me?"*
> — *Acts 9:4*

That was Jesus.

And that one encounter changed everything.

Blindness struck Saul for three days, until a believer named Ananias prayed for him and he recovered his sight. From that moment on, Saul became Paul, and instead of persecuting Christians, he became one of their most passionate leaders.

Paul abandoned his status and comfort and embarked on missionary journeys throughout the Roman Empire, from Jerusalem to Asia Minor, from Macedonia to Greece, and even to Rome. He preached in synagogues, taught in homes, debated philosophers in Athens, and planted churches across the known world.

And he suffered for it.

Paul was stoned by people, beaten with rods, whipped, shipwrecked, and imprisoned. He wrote many of his letters, now part of the New Testament, while in chains. In Rome, they executed him, giving his life for the One he had once opposed.

Paul had it easy. He had prestige. He had everything this world could offer. But he laid it all down when he met Jesus.

Why?

Because he knew salvation wasn't the end of the road, it was the start of a mission.

The First Call to Action

In Acts 2, Peter stands up before the crowd at Pentecost, filled with the Holy Spirit, and delivers the message that would birth the early Church. He tells them the truth plainly: that Jesus, whom they crucified, is both Lord and Messiah. And when the people are "cut to the heart," they ask the same question:

"What shall we do?"

And Peter replies:

"Repent and be baptized, every one of you, in the name of Jesus Christ for the forgiveness of your sins. And you will receive the gift of the Holy Spirit."
— *Acts 2:38*

He didn't say, "Just wait for heaven." He said Repent, be baptized, and receive the Holy Spirit. Why? There is a mission now. A purpose. A kingdom being built, and we're invited to be part of it.

A Spirit-Filled Life is a Powerful Life

Peter continues by quoting the prophet Joel:

"In the last days, God says, I will pour out my Spirit on all people... Your sons and daughters will prophesy... I will show wonders... And everyone who calls on the name of the Lord will be saved."
— *Acts 2:17–21*

That prophecy wasn't just for the apostles. It's for us. Right now.

We are living in these "last days." The Spirit is still being poured out. God is still empowering ordinary people with extraordinary authority, not just to survive this world, but to bring heaven to earth.

Spiritual Authority: You Were Made for Battle

So, what now? If you're saved, forgiven, and filled with the Spirit… what does that mean for your daily life?

It means you've been equipped for battle.

"The weapons we fight with are not the weapons of the world. On the contrary, they have divine power to demolish strongholds."
— 2 Corinthians 10:4–5

You are not weak. You are not without direction. You carry authority in Jesus' name.

"I have given you authority to trample on snakes and scorpions and to overcome all the power of the enemy; nothing will harm you."

— Luke 10:19

A passive faith was never your intended way of life. The Holy Spirit doesn't just comfort; you are commissioned. You were called not just to be saved from something, but to be saved for something.

The Two Most Important Commandments

"'Love the Lord your God with all your heart and with all your soul and with all your mind.' This is the first and greatest commandment. And the second is like it: 'Love your neighbor as yourself.' All the Law and the Prophets hang on these two commandments."

— Matthew 22:37–40

Your calling isn't just about preaching from a pulpit or being a missionary overseas (though for some it may be). Wherever you are is your calling. Your family. The area where you live. Your workplace.

The world is full of lies that sound like light.

That's why we placed you here, to expose the lie and reflect the true Light.

To speak the truth in love.

To pray with authority.

To serve with compassion.

To live unshaken in a shaking world.

You were born into this time, not by accident, but by divine design.

You've been given truth.

You've been given grace.

You've been given power of the Spirit.

What Now?

Now, we go.

Not just to church, but into the world.

Not just to be safe, but to be bold.

Not just to wait, but to fight.

This is not the end of the story. This is the start of your calling.

Let the Holy Spirit lead you.

Let the Word of God guide you.

Let your life answer the question the world is silently asking: "Is there any hope?"

And with your words, your love, your power in Christ, may your life resound with this answer: Yes, there is hope.

His name is <u>Jesus.</u>

Final Word

This book's purpose wasn't entertainment or debate, but awakening. You have seen the pattern. You've heard the warnings. You have glimpsed hope. Now the choice is yours.

Don't just read this message; respond to it.

"But if serving the Lord seems undesirable to you, then choose for yourselves this day whom you will serve... But as for me and my household, we will serve the Lord."

— *Joshua 24:15*

Testimonies and Source Material

Books and Authors

- **Howard Pittman** – *Placebo*
  Firsthand account of Pittman's near-death experience involving a confrontation with the devil and a vision of the lukewarm church.
- **Howard Storm** – *My Descent Into Death*
  Autobiographical account of Storm's transition from atheism to Christianity following a harrowing NDE in which beings of light turned violent before he cried out to Jesus.
- **Randy Kay** – *Revelations from Heaven*
  Features Kay's clinically verified NDE and his encounter with Jesus, resulting in repentance and a calling to ministry.
- **Ray Comfort** – *God Has a Wonderful Plan for Your Life*
  Apologetic work that emphasizes the use of the moral law to awaken the conscience and the courtroom analogy to explain salvation.
- **Lee Strobel** – *The Case for Christ & The Case for Miracles*
  Journalistic investigations into the historical evidence for Jesus Christ, miracles, and personal testimonies validating supernatural experiences.
- **John Burke** – *Imagine Heaven*
  Comprehensive exploration of NDEs, comparing accounts with biblical teachings to provide insights into life after death and the reality of heaven.

Testimony Channels & Media

- **Randy Kay Ministries** (YouTube)
  Interviews featuring testimonies of heaven, hell, and post-death encounters through a biblical lens.
- **Touching the Afterlife** (YouTube)
  A channel sharing diverse NDE testimonies.
- **God's Voice Today** (YouTube)
  Both platforms regularly feature NDEs and conversion testimonies from ex-New Age practitioners and spiritual seekers.
- **The Shawn Ryan Show** – *Inside the Demonic World with an Exorcist (Episode #141)*
  Interview with **Father Dan Reehil**, a Catholic exorcist, sharing chilling but well-documented accounts of possession and spiritual warfare.
- **Tomi Arayomi** (YouTube)
  Prophetic ministry channel discussing contemporary spiritual experiences, dreams, and visions with biblical discernment and prophetic insights.

Ex-New Age and Deliverance Testimonies

- **Jenn Nizza** – Former psychic medium, now Christian speaker and host of *Ex-Psychic Saved Podcast* speaks extensively on New Age deception and mediumship through her books and interviews.
- **Angela Ucci (formerly Scafidi)** – Former astrologer and New Age teacher

Now a born-again Christian and co-host of *Heaven & Healing Podcast*, sharing insights on spiritual deception and biblical truth.

Apologetics & Biblical Discernment

- **Living Waters / Way of the Master** – Ray Comfort's YouTube ministry Evangelistic teachings focused on sin, repentance, and salvation through Christ.
- **GotQuestions.org** – Theologically sound explanations to common biblical and spiritual questions.
- **Bible Gateway** – Scripture citations and word studies used for biblical cross-referencing.

Note: These resources were either directly cited or used as background research in the development of this book. Inclusion does not imply agreement on all points, but rather reflects key contributions to the topics discussed.

All testimonies and experiences cited in this book are publicly available and attributed to their original speakers. The author has made every effort to accurately reflect their accounts. Where applicable, direct quotes and paraphrases are used with respect and care. No affiliation or endorsement is implied.

Fair Use & Testimony Reference Disclaimer

This book includes references to publicly available testimonies, interviews, and content from individuals including, but not limited to, Howard Storm, Randy Kay, Jenn Nizza, Angela Ucci, and others. These references are cited for the purposes of religious commentary, theological reflection, and education, in accordance with the principles of fair use under United States copyright law (17 U.S.C. § 107).

Every effort has been made to accurately represent their public accounts and attribute proper credit. No endorsement or affiliation is implied by the mention of any individual, and all rights to original material remain with their respective creators and publishers.